Got Debt?

Reduce Your Debt,
Improve Your Credit,
&
Learn to Use Debt Wisely

Benjamin J. Miller

ISBN-13:   **978-1470004118**

ISBN-10:   **1470004119**

For information on licensing
content, special discounts for mass
purchases, receiving the author at a
live event, or direct financial advice,
visit Benjamin J. Miller directly at:

www.ithinkaboutmoney.com

And on Facebook, at:

www.facebook.com/ithinkaboutmoney

This book is dedicated to my mother, who not only started me on the road to financial intelligence, but kept me on it[1].

---

[1] In much the same way as she helped me learn to drive, by repeatedly saying "Watch out!!" before finally putting her head in her hands and praying. Love you Mom ☺

<u>TO YOU, THE READER</u>

I wrote this book to provide you with financial knowledge and insight, and a few laughs as well. Just remember, laughing about money can be the first step to thinking about it, and thinking about it leads to taking action.

I have used the steps in this book successfully for my own debts, and I have taught others to do this as well. It can be done, and the smile on someone's face when you've saved them a lot of money is a beautiful thing[1].

Enjoy!

---

[1] If these steps work for you, like my facebook page and post your own smile! www.facebook.com/ithinkaboutmoney

<u>Caveat - Part 1</u>

Benjamin J. Miller is not an Accountant or Attorney and any advice pertaining to tax or legal matters should be discussed with professionals of this type before action is taken[1].

---

[1] For example, if you stop filing your tax return or start assaulting your creditors because you thought I said those were good ideas, I'm not responsible.

<u>Caveat – Part 2</u>

Besides that, I'm not even an accredited Financial Planner! I have the silly notion that the measuring level for those who teach about investing and finance shouldn't be based primarily on what they've learned to sell[1], but rather their actual skill in investing, which should be reflected in their own personal finances and lifestyle[2]. Strange thoughts perhaps, but these principles have helped me determine who to listen to, and so I share them with you.

---

[1] Such as insurance and mutual funds, the keystones of many Financial Planners' programs for creating wealth. Is this because they're the best methods available, or because the Planners are generally trained by companies in those industries who offer commissions on those products? I wonder…

[2] After all, do you really want dietary lessons from someone who is seriously overweight and can't stop eating? Sounds funny, but many people have as financial advisors those who continue to make more money *advising*, than they do *investing*.

Caveat – Part 3

P.S. For any financial planners (or companies who train them) who were offended by that last page, I obviously didn't mean you.

P.P.S. Every time I read that last caveat it seems harsher. I <u>like</u> the idea of financial planning, and people <u>should</u> feel comfortable seeking outside help with their finances. Just know where your advisor's experience comes from, where their compensation comes from, most importantly where their own <u>money</u> comes from, and judge their advice accordingly.

<u>Table of Contents</u>

What This Book Is About

Cash is king. This is a phrase many of you have heard again and again, and it's particularly true when you need some. This book is about bringing you new ways of putting cash in your pocket. All of these ways involve a little bit of work, but more importantly, they involve a lot of thinking. When you think more, you work less.

This particular book is about debt. Not focused on all kinds of debt. Just one kind. The bad kind. The kind you hate. Debt here today will be treated like the biggest, ugliest, nastiest cockroach[1] you ever saw. And we will step on it accordingly. Firmly, and with relish[2].

---

[1] Married people may substitute the word 'in-law' for cockroach here, if it helps.

[2] Again, for the married, stepping on in-laws should be performed by professionals. Don't try this at home.

First, we will explain and identify bad debt, hereafter referred to as BD. Not to be confused with either BO or VD, although making that sort of mental connection may encourage you to get rid of it quicker, so by all means go ahead. There's a lot to know about BD; what BD means, how it affects us, and the choices we make every day to either perpetuate it or exterminate it.

Next, we will examine the roots of BD. How it starts, what it feeds on, and the reasons you're most likely to have it.

Finally, we will show you how to conquer BD, and create cash! This is the first step in the Cash Equation.

$$\mathbf{BD(0)} = \underline{B}ad \ \underline{D}ebt \ x \ Zero^{[1]}$$

---

[1] Which means it becomes zero in case you didn't know. No biggie, this is about as complex as the math gets in this book.

The full equation[1] is:

$$BD(0) + MSI(SA + HA - GD) + AA(\infty) - T = \$\$$$

Don't get scared, this is just a teaser for future concepts. We're only talking about the first part BD(0) in this book. Bonus points if you can figure out what all (or even any of) the letters stand for before I tell you. It helps if you remember it's a conceptual equation, not a mathematical one. I'll give you one hint: T should also be very close to zero.

Guesses can be submitted through

www.ithinkaboutmoney.com

If I'm really impressed with you, you might get my next book for free!

Let's get started!

---

[1] As it stands today. This equation can be changed or modified as I learn more, or as I desire to write more books whether I've learned anything new or not. You'll just have to take your chances.

"Debt can turn a free, happy person into a bitter human being."

-Michael Mihalik

<u>What Is BD?</u>

DO NOT SKIP THIS CHAPTER!

I say this not because I need you to read every word of mine for some personal ego boost. Trust me, my ego is so well-boosted, it's constantly buffeted by solar winds. Nor is it for any personal monetary gain, because, hey, you already bought/borrowed/begged/stole the book. It's for you. Be honest with yourself. If you knew everything about debt, you wouldn't be reading this book. Since you are, make the most of it. Get as much knowledge from it as you can…even if it means reading a few things you might have heard before. Repetition is good.

Before we can talk about Bad Debt, first we have to define debt. Debt is what is due, or owed, from one to another. Debt is an obligation. Obligation is a good word. It's not a bad thing to be obligated to someone. It means that they did something for you that you feel obliged to repay. That's good. May you feel obligated to more and more people over time, because that means more and more people are helping you.

That being said, debt does have a dark side[1]. Here it is. It's very simple. Pay close attention. This is the theme of the book I am giving you here. Ready?

Bad Debt is debt YOU have to pay for.

It's easiest to explain this by showing an example of Good Debt here. If you can borrow money at a rate of, say 2% (meaning if you borrow $1,000 at the end of the year you owe the lender $1,020), and lend it to others at a rate of, say 6% (meaning at the end of the year they owe you $1,060), this is good debt. It may seem like a strange example to some, but others will recognize this as how most banks do business. They give account holders a lower percentage in interest to lend out money to

---

[1] Yes, like the force. It chokes you, controls the weak-minded, and the IRS probably has a death star somewhere, I'm sure.

borrowers at a higher percentage. The lesson here: Be like the bank.

BD is when you take out that loan for a new car. It's when you rack up charges on your credit cards for shopping and eating out and the latest clothes and all the other stuff this material world makes you think you need. Don't get me wrong; I use my credit cards all the time. I think new cars, vacations; new clothes and eating out are all great! You can have all of that stuff **without** the guilt and financial problems, if you can control your money. And the first step in that means eliminating BD.

I'm constantly amazed when people I meet can complain to me about their money troubles, and then tell me about the new toys they bought in the same conversation! Just like the connection between fat and food, debt and spending go together. You don't get one without the other.

Bad Debt is anything you owe for things that didn't help you to grow. Owe to grow. Taking a loan out for education, for a business, for an investment, these can potentially be good debts[1]. Those things can help you grow, financially and in other ways. Even though they will still be a burden, these debts can more than pay for themselves over time. Sometimes you can even get debt to start paying for itself the moment you acquire it! That not only makes you feel better about your debt, it makes the people who loan you the money feel better about your debt as well. We'll explore the positives of good debt at a later date. Just remember for now that obligating yourself to the right people[2] for the right things can be very good.

---

[1] But don't take the loans yet; read my book on Good Debt first.
[2] Examples of the wrong people include bookies, 'family' men, and anyone with an 'indecent proposal'.

"A billion here, a billion there, pretty soon you're talking about real money."

- Everett Dirksen

What Does BD Really Cost You?

Here's a quick update on where we stand with
BD as a country and as individuals:

In 2011, the Federal Reserve calculated that the
US had about $2.43 TRILLION in consumer
debt (debt that is not secured by real estate).
This works out to every man, woman, and child
owing more than $8,000 apiece[1]. This number
continues to increase.

The portion of this that is considered *revolving
debt* (which basically means credit card debt) is
$793 BILLION.

According to recent data, 60% of credit card
users do not pay their balances off monthly.

---

[1] Try telling your kids they owe $8,000. That's a lot of Girl Scout
cookies, papers delivered, and lawns mowed.

The average interest rate on credit cards in 2011 was 14.72%[1].

This means....wait for it....in 2011 we paid as a country more than $70 BILLION IN INTEREST ON OUR CREDIT CARDS ALONE!!![2] That's an annual household average of **$2,325.61** you personally pay in interest that you'll never get back. No wonder they never stop sending you new credit card offers! This doesn't take into account late fees, balance transfer fees, annual fees, and all the other nickel-and-dime stuff. It also doesn't look at car loans, boat loans, and other fixed-payment loans.

The absolute worst of these come in 2 forms: Payday Loans and Tax Refund Loans. NEVER, EVER, EVER[3] take one of these loans. The interest rates here can be as high as **300%**, so that $1,000 you owe can turn into owing $3,000, to owing $9,000, to owing $27,000...disgusting right?

---

[1] All of this math is leading somewhere, I promise.

[2] Sorry for shouting, but I feel like a raised voice is needed here.

[3] Raising my voice again but in the next sentence you'll understand why.

Let's give some examples of better uses for this money. Instead of paying interest to credit card companies and the like you could do one of the following every year just by holding onto that average household amount:

1) Get all the cable channels and pay-per-view.
2) Get the game console system of your choice along with 3-4 games per month.
3) Cover your first month, last month, and security deposit to move into a new place[1].
4) Get 3 months of free groceries for you and your family.
5) Cover at least a month's rent, several months of utilities, fix up your house, take a family vacation, etc.

Are you motivated to get rid of your BD now?

---

[1] This one doesn't apply to anyone in New York City, unless perhaps you're moving into a closet.

*"The more I study the wealthy...
in an effort to learn how to help
more people around the world
become one of them...I'm
stunned by how many people are
actually not rich."*

- David Bach

The Roots of BD, and Our Biggest Challenges in Fixing It:

But why are we like this? How did we get into these bad habits in the first place? Oh there might have been one or even several bad things that happened to us financially[1], but these things can usually be overcome on our own. No, the real problems are why we never seem to have any reserve money for those emergencies[2], or why our bills seem to be constantly threatening to overwhelm us.

Listen up, because this may hurt. The most compelling reason most of us can't handle money well is because our friends and family (the strongest sources of influence in our life) don't handle money well. Or worse yet, they

---

[1] Like the time that vacuum salesperson came to the door, or when that Nigerian prince promised us so sincerely through email we could have his millions if we just gave him our bank account #. Nasreem, I will find you!

[2] And no, I don't mean when Best Buy or Payless Shoes has a 2 for 1 sale.

do handle money well but don't feel comfortable telling us about it. And before you tell me about rich uncle so-and-so, take a close look at everyone you spend time with or get advice from. Do they have BD? Can they afford what they want when they want it? Do they enjoy their career, or feel trapped? Have they retired young? Retired rich? When money comes up, do they focus on problems, or opportunities? Can they talk about money? Are they <u>happy</u> about money?

That last question is I think the most important. Whether you're poor or wealthy, if you're generally unhappy when you talk about money you're not using it right. It's there to help us and enable us to do things we couldn't have done without it, not to be a source of stress or discomfort. And believe it or not, you can be happy about debt! Strange as it may seem, <u>I wanted to owe one million dollars before I made one million dollars</u>…just because that was the way I was planning on making it[1].

---

[1] That last sentence might have made your brain hurt, and if so take a few deep breaths (or eat some chocolate) and read on. It's a topic for another book.

Regardless of where it came from, right now it's all about BD, and the way to be happy about BD is to get rid of it. I'm not suggesting you have to make new friends or get a new family[1], just be aware of where people are coming from when you hear their advice. The key points that I am making are best summed up here:

Money should be a happy topic, and chocolate makes your brain hurt less[2].

Keep in mind, you're reading this book because you want to get control of your debt and you're looking for ways to do it. I won't waste time telling you any more whys...when what we really should be focusing on are the hows.

---

[1] These suggestions are indeed made by other books of this type, but personally I think the devil you know is safer. Who knows what hell new friends (much less new family) might put you through? *shiver*

[2] Ok, maybe it's a placebo effect, but I. Just. Don't. Care.

"Winners keep score."

- Anonymous

Your Credit Score
Part 1: The Report

Your credit score is your financial blood pressure. Proper management of it is very important to your overall well-being, but it takes time to make lasting changes. So for right now, we're just going to take a quick reading. Here's how you do that:

1) Roll up your sleeve
2) Make a fist (around your phone or mouse)
3) Call (877)322-8228, or visit

www.annualcreditreport.com

This is a way to request your FREE[1] copy of your credit **report**. Everyone is allowed a FREE[2] copy of their credit **report** from each of the 3 credit reporting firms (TransUnion,

---

[1] Yes, I really mean FREE. No charges, fees, programs to sign up for, shipping & handling, or costs of any kind.

[2] Yes, really. FREE! I'm sure. Yes I checked. Ok, I'll check again. Yup. Still FREE.

Experian, and Equifax) once a year. Since there are 3 different companies that **report** your credit, make sure you get a FREE[1] **report** from each one every year.

The reason I keep bolding the word **report**, is because you're not actually getting your credit **score**. If you want your credit **score**, you can pay[2] for it (using this same website if you want), or you can contact a bank lender/mortgage broker you trust to get it for you[3]. Usually this second way can be done at no expense, but you need to give your Social Security number, so be careful. Remember, the **report** is more useful right now.

Once you've ordered or downloaded your credit **reports**, <u>leave them alone</u>. That's right. We'll work on them later if needed, but for most people with BD (even those with bad credit),

---

[1] Yes, I know it's amazing. Yes, I know very few things are truly FREE anymore. If it makes you feel better, you probably paid for this information by buying my e-book. Oh, you got it as a gift? Well then, send me some money so you feel better.

[2] Yes, yes, I know that part isn't FREE. Wait, there's still a way to get it FREE, keep reading.

[3] He/she is going to want to hear you want to buy property. You do. Whether its today or not, doesn't matter ☺

the credit report is the last thing to work on, not the first. I wanted you to order them now because they take some time if ordered by mail, and we will get to them eventually.

Note: I am not personally involved with the annual credit reporting service, and their terms may change. I currently use this service myself, and I recommend it to my clients. If you suspect any or all of your BD comes from **identity theft**, this should be addressed right away. The website above has links for reporting such activity and setting up alerts to prevent it.

Getting Started

Ok. Deep breath. You already know you have BD. I'm not going to make you tell your parents, your friends, the people you work with, or anyone else until you're ready. But you have to be completely honest with yourself.

No doctor, mechanic, lawyer, engineer, contractor or any other professional worth their salt will ever tell you what should be done until they've done a full examination[1], and self-exams are recommended often. This is where you start.

You want to create a debt picture. This picture is a snapshot of your current debt, as accurate as possible to where it stands today. Never mind what it will be like tomorrow, next week,

---

[1] Fortunately the one in this book doesn't require you to remove any clothing, sign any binding documents, or listen hard for that rattling noise you could have sworn you heard just this morning when you started it up.

next month, or next year. You can update it when you're ready, but you need to start now.

Your debt picture has several elements, and can easily be created on paper, in a computer text document, or a spreadsheet (the last one is best if you can use them). It should show the following:

1) <u>Each creditor[1], your BO[2] (Balance Owed) and your AC (Available Credit)</u>.

2) <u>The interest rate you are paying</u>. If you are paying different interest rates on different amounts to the same creditor, go back to step 1 and list the creditor more than once.

3) <u>Your minimum payment</u>, which for most people is the critical number.

4) <u>Your terms</u> - How many months remaining for fixed payment loans, whether payment arrangements or rates

---

[1] Fancy word for people you owe money to. You can substitute the term "bloodsucking leech" if you prefer.

[2] Another great abbreviation to free-associate with. No one wants BO, do they?

will change at a future date, etc. For credit cards, know that minimum payments usually range between 2% - 4% of your total balance, which of course does little or nothing to the principal, ensuring that you will pay tens of thousands of dollars in interest before the balance is gone[1].

There's an example of how this all breaks down on paper over the next 2 pages.

---

[1] Keep smiling, keep breathing. There's a light at the end of the tunnel, and it's not a train.

SAMPLE DEBT PICTURE

Here are the terms (below), and then examples of how they would look with an average amount of revolving debt.

C - Creditor   **BO - Balance Owed**
R - Rate   **AC – Avail. Credit**
T - Terms   **MP - Min. Payment**

C Reward Credit Card 1 **BO** $2,000
R 13.99% **AC** $1,000
T Standard. **MP** $60

C Retail Credit Card 2 **BO** $3,000
R 14.99% **AC** $1,000
T Standard. **MP** $90

C Bank Credit Card 3 **BO** $5,000
R 15.99% **AC** $0
T Standard. **MP** $150

C Bank Credit Card 3a **BO** $5,000
R 5.99% **AC** $0
T Intro rate for 12mths **MP** $150

C Auto Loan **BO** $12,000
R 8% **AC** $0
T 12/60 payments made. **MP** $243

C School Loan **BO** $25,000
R 4% **AC** $0
T 24/96 payments made. **MP** $305

Totals:
$52,000 in Balance Owed
$998 in Monthly Payments
10.5% Average Interest Rate

Numbers are slightly rounded; obviously your individual picture will look slightly different. The monthly payment number above assumes you are only making the minimum payment on your credit cards, which would mean a repayment period of **more than 30 years**. Of course, that's only if you don't charge anything more on these cards. We'd like to improve on this.[1]

---

[1] Ya think??

<u>SAMPLE DEBT PICTURE - EXPLAINED</u>

Ok, let's go over that picture a bit. So on the first credit card, you owe $2,000 and have $1,000 in available credit. The interest rate is 13.99%, and I used an average 3% of the amount owed to calculate the minimum payment. Standard terms because nothing changes, you make your payment monthly.

Not much is different for the others, except the 3rd credit card has 2 balances with different rates for each. One of those special balance transfer checks got mailed to you and you used it for a lower interest rate[1], but that rate only lasts for a short term. The auto loan and school loan have larger payments because those pay

---

[1] While spending more money most likely, this is why they send you those checks all the time.

off more of the principal[1], and there you know how many payments you have left.

Finally there are the totals. Knowing how much debt you have is important, as well as your ongoing payment amounts, but the key number here is really the average interest rate. That number is going to make the difference between paying off these debts over a lifetime, or knocking them over like dominoes by paying off one and then applying the paid off card's minimum payment to the next.

Now that you have your debt picture, what do you do with it? There are a number of things we can do to improve it, but before we get to that point there's one thing that's much more important. Seems silly really, that I even have to mention it, but I will. I'll even go on to another chapter explaining the how and why of this. Ready? Here it is.

DON'T ADD TO IT!

---

[1] Meaning unlike the credit cards, you might pay these loans off in less time than a mortgage.

"You cannot keep out of trouble by spending more than you earn."

— **Abraham Lincoln**

<u>Living Within Your Means</u>

I've read a lot of books about money and wealth management. Without contradicting them, I'm just going to say that some advice works better at one level of education, and some advice works better at another level. Speaking plainly, I've seen that it's hard for someone who's deep in Bad Debt to suddenly think like a rich person, even when they suddenly come into money. Don't be the lottery winner who goes bankrupt.

Here are the three basic debt-related lifestyles as I see them:

1) **Living above your means**
2) **Living within your means**
3) **Living beneath your means**

These are listed in order as to how people generally progress (if they're improving).

Far too many of us are in the first group; we spend too much, too often, on things we don't need[1]. The third group is where most wealthy people find themselves; actually having the problem of more money coming in than they know what to do with[2]. There are also some financially unhealthy people in the third group, for whom spending even a single dollar frivolously is cause for *seppuku*[3]. The second group is where I want to focus, since for most this is the true challenge.

Living within your means has 3 parts to it, 2 of which most people never think of until it's too late. The first part is easy (to say, at least), that of **making sure your income exceeds your expenses**. If you're already working full-time, the best way to work on this is by cutting your

---

[1] If you're going to start on how you need everything you spend money on, you better follow that up by telling me how much SPAM, Ramen Noodles, Water (Tap), and Rice you ate this month. If you ate outside your house in the past 90 days, have cable television, and/or got clothing recently from somewhere other than the nearest thrift shop, methinks you might be able to scrimp a teensy bit more.

[2] Yes I know it's a disgusting situation to imagine, and I only hope we can all experience it to see how disgusting it is first-hand.

[3] It means ritual disembowelment. It's very bad for you, and you'll never get those stains out of the carpeting.

expenses. The most significant way to do this is coming up shortly. The second part is, **create a reserve account for emergencies**. "But Ben," you might say, "you mean I should save money for bad things that haven't happened yet, things I don't even expect <u>will</u> happen?" YES! Bad things happen, expect them ahead of time and be pleasantly surprised if they don't.

<u>Your reserve should have 6 months of your expenses in it</u>. This gives you time to: Look for a new job, recover from an illness, take care of a loved one, fix your car or house, etc. If you don't have a reserve account like this, start creating one immediately, and once you have it, don't touch it[1]. Part three is about **starting an investment account**, but when you're drowning it's not the time to save for a boat, so we'll get to that in a later book.

---

[1] Except for…umm….well….EMERGENCIES! Just checking to see if you remembered.

__Debt Management – Part 1__

Cutting expenses is always a tough thing to do, but the beauty of managing your debt is that sometimes <u>you can keep the exact same lifestyle you've been living, while paying your bills off quicker, just by making some phone calls</u>. Most people don't fully understand this, are not making these calls, or don't know what to say, and its costing them thousands of dollars every year.

First off, let me tell you there are many companies & agencies that can help you with this. Some are legitimate, some are not. Some charge, others don't. Some will do a better job than you would, and some can actually make your situation worse. Use these people only if you know you won't do it yourself[1]. If you can take the time to work on this yourself, you'll

---

[1] Just make sure it's before calling Louie the Leg-Breaker or pricing out that kidney on E-bay. BAD!

have better long-lasting results, because as long as you have debt of any kind, you will want to be managing it[1].

Managing your debt simply means <u>making sure the money you owe is at the lowest interest rates possible, with the best terms possible</u>. Since your goal is to get rid of BD, you want to create monthly payments you can afford, while at the same time paying off as much principal as you can each month.

Let's begin calling.

Working from your debt picture, start by contacting the customer service line of the company charging you the highest interest rate[2]. Be polite, and tell whoever you connect with you were hoping they could 'help you with something'. Explain that you are consolidating your debt, and feel free to mention that they are

---

[1] Good debt and Bad debt are like employees. GD is the one working hard to help you grow and expand, while BD is performing industrial espionage and writing funny-but-sad-cause-its-true cartoons about you behind your back. Motivate the former and execute the latter. This footnote is in no way inspired by Scott Adams. ☺

[2] Hold back the profanity, please.

currently charging you the highest interest rate out of all your creditors[1]. Tell them you want to continue using this account (a subtle hint that you may close it if you get better rates elsewhere), and ask for a re-evaluation of your interest rate.

At this point, some companies may tell you to await a letter informing you of their decision, or they may give you a lower interest rate on the spot. Whichever response you get, say thank you[2]. Make a note of your new rate, and then ask this follow-up question: "What balance transfer promotions are you running?"

---

[1] If you can't say this nicely, leave it out. Remember, customer service people are sensitive to 'bloodsucking leech' references.
[2] Yes, manners count when you're trying to get people to help save you money. If you're a rude person, you may want a friend to speak for you on these calls. If you can't do that, eat some chocolate first. It might put you in a better mood.

Balance Transfer Promotions

A few quick words about these before you get back to that phone call. You see, to many companies out there, debt is a product[1]. Like all products, it goes on sale occasionally…and the reason products go on sale[2] is so <u>they can get you to buy more than you normally would</u>. In this case however, we'll use the sales to our advantage.

Credit card debt can go on sale in the form of balance transfer promotions. These promotions can be offered by credit card companies you have an account with, as well as those you don't. Generally, a balance transfer promotion goes as follows: They offer you a very low rate (usually between 0% and 6%) for a specified period of time (anywhere from 6 months to 5 years), as long as you do the following:

---

[1] Like corn, cream cheese, or Chewbacca dolls (sorry, ran away with the alliteration there).
[2] Listen up Mom, this is for you.

A) Open a new account with them.

Or if you already have an account with them,

B) Transfer a balance from somewhere else to that account.

They will even include their own checks to use for these transfers[1]. Now, these promotions can be incredibly useful for people looking to pay down high interest rate debt. However, you MUST follow the rules they lay down when you accept the promotion. I cannot stress this enough. There are 2 basic rules that usually apply:

1) All payments MUST be made on time[2].
2) Any payment made to the company above your minimum payment will apply to higher-rate balances first, if there are any.

---

[1] Aren't they nice??
[2] Unlike non-promotional payments, where grace periods or lame excuses like 'my dog ate the bill' might save you.

The second rule isn't always in effect, and a way to avoid problems there is once you get a really good promotion going, don't use the card for anything else until the promotional balance is paid off.

Failing to follow these rules can result in more than just a much higher interest rate being immediately applied to whatever you still owe them. They can also charge you <u>as if you had been paying that higher rate from the beginning of the promotion!</u>[1] I do want you to use these, just follow the rules. Set up auto-deduct payments from your checking account if you can.

---

[1] That's like you signed up to pay 29.99% interest from day one instead of the 5% you thought you'd be paying. Not a happy moment, but remember this is only if you miss a payment.

Debt Management – Part 2

Let's get back to your phone call[1]. Make a note of whatever balance transfer promotions they're running...the rate, how much money you can transfer, and how long the rate lasts. The last question to ask is about your available credit. Request an increase of your credit line, (not to spend more!) only for the purpose of shifting other debt. You may end up shifting debt even without a special offer, just because one card's regular interest rate is lower than another and they've increased your credit line.

Make notes for everything, including the name and ID # of whoever you're speaking to (it helps to refer to this when you call back, you will most likely speak to someone else the next time). <u>Do not make a transfer yet</u>. Whatever offer they have isn't expiring tomorrow, wait until you've made all your calls first.

---

[1] You didn't leave them on hold while you read the last chapter did you? Good.

That's right, I said calls. Now that you've done the first one, the others should be easy. Call every creditor you have...credit card companies, auto loan lenders, education loan lenders, even the bank that holds your mortgage if you have one. With every creditor (except for the mortgage holder) the call will be the same as before...seeing if they will reduce your rate, asking about balance transfers, attempting to increase your available credit, and making notes for each.

If you have a mortgage, the call is slightly different. Mortgages and home equity loans are a completely different animal[1], and the ins and outs of how to properly use them will be covered in a different book. If you have a home loan already, you've already learned a bit about how they operate[2], so I'll just summarize your options here. If you don't own a home

---

[1] Just an expression...but think soft, cuddly rabbit instead of ferocious, man-eating tiger. Home loans are friends. Of course, a lot of people lately didn't take proper care of their rabbits, which later bit their heads off. It happens.

[2] Usually people learn from their mortgage broker or bank, which is kind of like the wolf teaching the sheep. At least talk to multiple 'wolves', so you can filter the sales-talk from the facts.

this might still be interesting if you ever plan to buy one.

First, if mortgage rates are similar or lower than they were when you got your loan originally, you may want to lower your rate or do what's called a cash-out refinance. The latter involves borrowing more on your home, and using the equity you've pulled out to pay off your higher-interest debt. If rates are higher now, the second option is to ask your mortgage lender about a home equity loan or home equity line of credit. The rates and terms they offer you with this sort of loan are often much better than credit cards, so it's worth exploring.

You'll notice I didn't discuss the possibility of you having property with no mortgage on it. Remember this: Lenders will generally loan you money on property at rates and terms you will never get elsewhere (also known as secured debt), so always borrow against property first. If you're lucky enough to have land or property that has no loans on it, immediately borrow against that to eliminate your BD…it will almost always be the right option.

Debt Management – Part 3

There is one last loan type to discuss[1] before you're done information-gathering. These are called Micro Loans.

This type of lending has grown strong roots in the internet community through sites like Prosper.com, which happens to be a site I have used personally and recommended to others.

The site functions like Ebay in that people from all over can bid on loans, or create their own listings for loans as I will now suggest to you. FYI, I have lent money through Prosper (as any individual can), but I have no ownership ties to them and other sites can provide this service as well.

---

[1] I've left out borrowing from family members for an important reason: You're not ready. Ask family members for money when you can show them how well you use yours, not how poorly you use yours. Don't spread BD.

The advantage of using this type of site is that it allows you to select what rate of interest you would like to pay.

On Prosper for example, once you have created your account as a borrower there it will assign you a letter grade representing your credit score, anywhere from HR (High Risk) up through AA. Then, you can look at a 30-day average for loan rates, and based on your credit grade and loan amount (on Prosper you can borrow between $1,000 and $25,000 currently) you can determine the average rate your listing is likely to get.

Important note: Prosper loans are principal and interest payments for 3 years, so its significantly different from credit cards in that you will pay this amount off.

Now that you've got all your information, make some decisions! Sell your debt to the lowest bidder[1]! Refinance, consolidate, pay off those higher interest cards, and watch your debt picture improve! Lower your monthly

---

[1] This is one case where selling low is actually a good thing.

payments if you need to, or just pay off more principal and less interest each month![1]

And the best part is[2], in 3 to 6 months you can do this over again and improve your picture even MORE!!![3]

---

[1] Ok that's the last exclamation for this chapter I promise; I'm just a little excited for you, ok?

[2] Uh oh, that last footnote might have been a lie...

[3] Ok. Really done now. All exclaimed out.

<u>SAMPLE DEBT PICTURE (Revised)</u>

C - Creditor   **BO - Balance Owed**
R - Rate   **AC – Avail. Credit**
T - Terms   **MP - Min. Payment**

C Reward Credit Card 1 **BO** $5,000
R 9.99%   **AC** $0
T Standard.   **MP** $150

C Retail Credit Card 2 **BO** $0
R 14.99%   **AC** $0
T Standard.   **MP** $0

C Bank Credit Card 3   **BO** $0
R 15.99%   **AC** $0
T Standard.   **MP** $0

C Bank Credit Card 3a   **BO** $5,000
R 5.99%   **AC** $0
T Intro rate for 12 mths. **MP** $150

C Auto Loan   **BO** $12,000
R 4%   **AC** $0
T 12/60 payments made.   **MP** $221

C School Loan   **BO** $25,000
R 4%   **AC** $0
T 24/96 payments made.   **MP** $305

C Prosper Loan   **BO** $5,000
R 8%   **AC** $0
T 0/36 payments made.   **MP** $157

Totals:
$52,000 in Balance Owed
$983 in Monthly Payments
6.5% Average Interest Rate

In our revised picture, we see first that credit
card #1 reduced its interest rate from 13.99%
down to 9.99%, after a nice conversation where
we reminded them of our long term credit
history with them, and especially of our recent

timely payments[1]. We also rolled the debt from credit cards #2 and #3 into a Prosper loan, going from 15.99% and 14.99% all the way down to 8%! Even better, that money will be paid off in 3 years now and our monthly payment went up by only $7.

If we didn't mind raising our monthly payment a little more, we could have rolled credit card #1 into the Prosper loan too, but this time we elected to keep monthly expenses low. The Auto Loan people (12 months of timely payments paid off) lowered their rate as well which lowered that payment by $22, so our net gain was $15 a month.

Any extra money at the end of the month will go towards paying off credit card #1, since that's the highest interest rate now. If you compare from the first debt picture, our average interest rate has gone from over 10% to under 7%, and the majority of these payments are principal and interest instead of interest-only.

---

[1] Smile when you say that.

That change will put more cash in your pocket every month as debts are paid off, which can be used to create or improve that reserve account, keep up with your expenses, pay off your other debts faster if needed, or even invest![1]

Add that to the advantage of continuing to live within your means while making timely payments and you'll see why it's worth revising this picture again in a few months. Those other credit cards you paid off will be back, offering even lower rates for you to shift some debt to them, which lowers your monthly payments further. It's a vicious cycle, in your favor! Say goodbye, BD!

---

[1] Remember, investing is a tricky topic too; fortunately I plan to write a lot more on this subject. Be patient ☺

Your Credit Score
Part 2: Improvement

Even though this book is primarily about BD and not your credit score, I thought a page or two here on it would be useful. Remember, BD is the enemy[1]...if you learn to *use debt wisely*, more people will want to lend to you at better rates and terms.

It's time to open up that credit report I told you to hide away earlier. You should have 3 of them by now, one from each credit reporting company. There are 3 areas I want you to look at:

Open accounts – This is important to check, because any open accounts (credit cards or loans) you don't remember setting up may be an indicator of identity theft. If the account is a year old or more, and there is no balance on it,

---

[1] Like in-laws and cockroaches, remember? Stay focused.

it may be something you set up and forgot[1]. If you're sure you won't use that account again in the future or you suspect identity theft, call the lender and close it.

Unpaid Balances (settled) – This means accounts you opened and didn't pay or paid very late, and the issue is now closed. The account may be open, but either you paid the money eventually in full, or they settled, or they wrote you off[2]. Either way, the fact that it still shows on your credit report means it's a black mark against you, and you should try to remove it[3].

Use the skills learned making your earlier calls to convince the lender that since the balance is now settled and you are working to restore your credit, you would be very appreciative if they contacted the credit reporting service and removed the item. The carrot that may help sweeten the deal for them is your desire to

---

[1] Retail store cards are very forgettable this way (they give you 10% off that day, but then you buy 20% more).

[2] It can happen with smaller amounts, but don't count on it. Businesses generally collect what they're owed, otherwise they'd be charities.

[3] 1 part bleach to 3 parts water, and voila! If only…

either continue doing business with them (if the account is still open) or your desire to renew doing business with them (if the account is since closed).

If you are polite and persistent, even just the word-of-mouth advantage for them should be enough. It may take several calls and/or letters (to the lender, to the credit reporting company to confirm after, etc.) to accomplish these things, but it's worth taking the time if you're planning on buying a house in the next 2 years or have other loans (Good Debt ones of course) you plan on getting.

Unpaid Balances (unsettled) – Guess what I'll recommend here? Settle them! Make contact with the lender. Suggest either a repayment plan you can afford or a one-time payment you can afford (in many cases the lender will settle for less in this situation). Then treat it as above to avoid a black mark.

LD - Not So Bad Debt[1]

As I said earlier, some advice works better at one level of education, and some advice works better at another level.

This book has been primarily focused on managing and eventually eradicating debt. However, since debt can be a very good thing when used wisely, let's take a moment to understand a good example of debt as a tool, referred to here as **Low-Interest Debt,** or **LD**.

Using LD as a tool to make you wealthy is based on a simple agreement you make with yourself.

Debt will be a part of your life.

If you don't agree with the above statement, it will be very hard for you to use debt to make you wealthy. It would also most likely be a

---

[1] Wait, what? Its ok, I'll explain.

denial of reality. Some people are actually able to live without debt, however when you think of all the ways debt is a part of your life and directly affects you, it's a lot harder to avoid than you might think. Some examples of debts that directly affect you that you probably don't think about are:

<u>Debts held by your workplace</u> – affects your job security, whether they can train you appropriately, whether they cut your pay or give you a raise, etc.

<u>Debts held by your school district</u> – affects your children and their education, how much your taxes will rise, how many fundraisers you'll be encouraged to support, etc.

<u>Debts held by your government</u>[1] – affects all levels of local and national services and programs that you depend on, including your workplace and school district from above.

---

[1] Don't get me started on this one. Imagine if you could borrow from a limitless bank account….well that's what governments seem to do. And we're all doing our best to work it off. Makes you want to be a King or Queen somewhere, right? ☺

What you are taxed on and for how much, as well as the cost of all the products and services that you pay for is heavily dependent on our local and national debts.[1]

So you see, even if you never owned a credit card again, or never borrowed from anyone directly again, you're still paying off debts and are directly affected by borrowing that many times you can't even say no to. With that understood, it becomes even more important to learn how to use debt to your advantage. This is simply the first step we're discussing. And this first step is:

Don't pay off LD faster than you need to.

It's that simple. If you have a low interest loan for school (the most common type) a car, a mortgage, or one of those balance transfer promotions like the examples from before, pay it off according to schedule and not one

---

[1] Did you ever check the finances of a company before going to work for them? What about the tax levels of a county or state before moving there? These things can have a huge impact on your life and overall happiness. That being said please don't move to Siberia just because the tax rate is low.

payment faster. Why? There are several reasons.

Reason #1 – **Make sure your reserve fund is full.** If you have a little extra every month but nothing solid in the bank, fill the reserve fund before paying off LD. Otherwise, you could end up with no debt but also no savings, which means the moment you have an unexpected expense you will have to take on debt fast, and that usually means a high interest rate[1]. Better to have LD and the reserve, so any emergencies are handled comfortably without adding new debt.

Reason #2 – **Tax advantages.** Some debts, like your mortgage, student loans, even small business loans, are a tax deduction which means that the interest rate you're paying is actually even lower than a loan with an equivalent rate. Again, if you pay these off quicker and then have to borrow from other places (like credit cards), you won't have the

---

[1] Remember those 'wrong people' I mentioned in an earlier footnote? Funny how they seem to pop up from everywhere the moment they know you're in a crisis.

same advantages and in the long run it will cost you much more.

Reason #3 – **Creating assets.** This last reason is just a glimpse into a larger world[1], but when you can create assets (businesses, property, loans that pay you, etc.), these assets will pay you higher rates of return than your LD is costing you.

If you're the slightest bit unsure about whether the debt you have is LD[2] (because not all mortgages, student loans, or car loans are and sometimes it can be hard to tell[3]) or you're just uncomfortable holding debt in general, only pay the minimum until your reserve fund is adequate. After it's appropriately filled, pay off any or all of your debts. Just because everyone around you borrows doesn't mean you have to. There is certainly a psychological satisfaction that comes from paying off a debt in its entirety.

---

[1] Just a peek. Don't try this at home, at least not until you've read more books.

[2] <u>Don't borrow just because the interest rate is low.</u> Student loan debt can be bad debt too; only take it if you need it. That PhD in Philosophy may not come in as handy as you think.

[3] This is where a good financial advisor comes in handy ☺

Epilogue

Thank you for reading this book. I know this information, if used correctly, can and will help bring BD to an end, not just for you but for others out there who are still struggling with it.

One last piece of advice: <u>If you see someone you want to pass this information on to, make them buy it</u>. I say this not out of greed[1], but simply because too many of us refuse to believe we should pay for financial education. Usually the ones who don't see its value are those who need it the most.

If you travel to a foreign country and don't learn the language, do you expect to get good prices? Of course not, yet we continue to be 'sheep taught by wolves' in our own country, letting those who financially profit from our decisions (both good and bad) educate us.

---

[1] Really. I don't expect these books to make me rich, especially because I've got other things that are already doing that ☺ Keep reading, I'll tell you all about them, I promise.

Most of us know that we should walk into a car dealership well prepared; banks are no different[1]. Pay early and up front for your knowledge, so you can avoid paying high-interest on your ignorance in the years to come. Words to live by.

Benjamin J. Miller
www.ithinkaboutmoney.com
www.facebook.com/ithinkaboutmoney

---

[1] Right down to the "Hmm, you drive a hard bargain. Let me check with my boss." Sound familiar?

*"A journey of a thousand miles
must begin with a single step."*

- Lao Tzu

GOT DEBT CHECKLIST[1] & STARTING WORKSHEET[2]

1. Order your 3 credit reports via phone or online.

2. Create your debt picture using the worksheet on the next two pages.

3. Make your first exploratory calls to your creditors. Take notes.

4. Investigate micro loans.

5. Negotiate, and then sell your debt to the lowest bidder(s).

6. Create your revised debt picture.

7. Make timely payments, keep a calendar of when debts are paid, and repeat the process in 3 to 6 months.

---

[1] The list seems simple enough, but there's a reason this is a book and not a flyer. Refer to the appropriate chapters while you do this, and don't be afraid to ask a professional for help if needed.
[2] Extra worksheets are at the back of the book.

C - Creditor   **BO - Balance Owed**
R - Rate   **AC – Avail. Credit**
T - Terms   **MP - Min. Payment**

1. C _____   BO $_____

    R _____   AC $_____

    T _____   MP $_____

2. C _____   BO $_____

    R _____   AC $_____

    T _____   MP $_____

3. C _____   BO $_____

    R _____   AC $_____

    T _____   MP $_____

4. C _____   BO $_____

    R _____   AC $_____

    T _____   MP $_____

5. C_____ BO $_____

   R_____ AC $_____

   T_____ MP $_____

6. C_____ BO $_____

   R_____ AC $_____

   T_____ MP $_____

7. C_____ BO $_____

   R_____ AC $_____

   T_____ MP $_____

Totals:

$_____ in Balance Owed

$_____ in Monthly Payments

_____% Average Interest Rate

References & Reviews - Websites

www.thesimpledollar.com a website that explains frugality in many easy to understand ways and offers everything from money-saving recipes to recommending games that teach your children about money too.

www.ivetriedthat.com a website that puts the wording 'tried and true' to the test by giving real accounts of different people's experiences with online jobs and other ways of making money, while exposing the scams along the way.

www.ithinkaboutmoney.com a website that encourages you to work with a financial advisor if you're not getting the results you want fast enough. Benjamin J. Miller is an investor who practices what he preaches, and he believes in teaching people how to think about money instead of just wishing they had more of it.

References & Reviews – Movies/TV

<u>FUN WITH DICK & JANE</u> is a light-hearted movie about real situations people experience when they lose their high paying jobs and have to make ends meet in other ways. Not meant as an instructional video.

<u>HOW I MET YOUR MOTHER –
SEASON 3, EPISODE 7</u> is a TV episode from a comedy series that's quite educational about the emotional roller-coaster married couples experience about debt and house-buying.[1]

<u>MAXED OUT</u> is a documentary film about banks and the credit card industry. It is eye-opening and heartfelt, and after you watch it you'll never look at plastic money (or the people that push it) the same way again.

---

[1] Dowisetrepla. Watch and learn.

References & Reviews - Books

<u>Automatic Millionaire, The</u>, by David Bach. A great book for those looking to set up systems that will eliminate their debt and turn their day-job savings into a retirement plan.

<u>Rich Dad, Poor Dad</u>, by Robert Kiyosaki. This is an excellent book for starting your financial education. It tells an interesting life story and provides the backbone for how to think like rich people do.

<u>My Next Book</u>, by Benjamin J. Miller. I've heard this book is going to be amazing[1], with Miller's classic blend of financial expertise and zany[2], off-the-wall humor. You'll laugh, you'll cry, you'll get rich![3]

---

[1] Toot, toot! Yup, that's my horn. Actual title is subject to change.
[2] I just like this word. It's great for Scrabble too.
[3] Absolutely no guarantees are implied here. You might not laugh or cry even once. Past laughter or tears at my jokes are not predictive of future results.

"You cannot spend your way out of recession or borrow your way out of debt."[1]

- Daniel Hannan

---

[1] Governments, are you listening??

<u>CALL TO ACTION</u>

Thank you for reading, now go get your bad debt under control! Share this book with others, and share your success stories with me to help me motivate others!

<u>www.ithinkaboutmoney.com</u>
<u>www.facebook.com/ithinkaboutmoney</u>[1]

---

[1] Like the Facebook page and you will be first to hear about discounts, upcoming books, and any other pieces of useful knowledge I might have to share.

<u>Acknowledgements</u>

Special thanks and recognition to some of those who have inspired and/or advised me:

Gary, one of the first people to receive this advice, which inspired me to share it with others. I hope you continue to share your gifts with the world, while remembering to enjoy the fruits of your labors.

Todd, my brother and business advisor

Sue, my good friend and editor

Matt, my real-estate advisor, realtor, and business partner

Mr. Levitz, my teacher.

My family and friends as a whole, for being supportive and encouraging of what has turned out to be a series of decidedly unconventional choices regarding my life.

My life has been enriched by knowing you all, and I appreciate that more than you know.

Also a note of thanks to Robert Kiyosaki, who started me down this path with his games and books, and Ben, who brought him to my attention.

There are many others I haven't mentioned whose contributions and impacts on my life are still quite significant. I'll just have to write more, but in the meantime –

Thank you.

<u>About The Author</u>

Benjamin J. Miller has a degree in Psychology, and his working experience following studies has focused on Advertising Sales and Sales Management for companies such as AOL/Time Warner and Thompson West Publishing.

Since 2004 he has owned and managed his own businesses and investments, and shortly after this began to share his knowledge with others. On January 31st 2005 he left his day job and began living off of these investments, and his life has never been the same since.

APPENDIX A:
EXTRA WORKSHEETS[1]

---

[1] These should last you quite awhile, but if you run out and your photocopier or scanner conks out (or if you just prefer to do this on computer), check back with me at www.ithinkaboutmoney.com, I may leave a downloadable spreadsheet there at some point.

C - Creditor   **BO - Balance Owed**
R - Rate   **AC – Avail. Credit**
T - Terms   **MP - Min. Payment**

1. **C** _____ **BO** $_____

   R _____ **AC** $_____

   T _____ **MP** $_____

2. **C** _____ **BO** $_____

   R _____ **AC** $_____

   T _____ **MP** $_____

3. **C** _____ **BO** $_____

   R _____ **AC** $_____

   T _____ **MP** $_____

4. **C** _____ **BO** $_____

   R _____ **AC** $_____

   T _____ **MP** $_____

5. C_____ BO $_____

   R_____ AC $_____

   T_____ MP $_____

6. C_____ BO $_____

   R_____ AC $_____

   T_____ MP $_____

7. C_____ BO $_____

   R_____ AC $_____

   T_____ MP $_____

Totals:

$_____ in Balance Owed

$_____ in Monthly Payments

_____% Average Interest Rate

C - Creditor   **BO - Balance Owed**
R - Rate   **AC – Avail. Credit**
T - Terms   **MP - Min. Payment**

1. C _____   BO $_____

   R _____   AC $_____

   T _____   MP $_____

2. C _____   BO $_____

   R _____   AC $_____

   T _____   MP $_____

3. C _____   BO $_____

   R _____   AC $_____

   T _____   MP $_____

4. C _____   BO $_____

   R _____   AC $_____

   T _____   MP $_____

5. C _____ BO $_____

   R _____ AC $_____

   T _____ MP $_____

6. C _____ BO $_____

   R _____ AC $_____

   T _____ MP $_____

7. C _____ BO $_____

   R _____ AC $_____

   T _____ MP $_____

Totals:

$_____ **in Balance Owed**

$_____ **in Monthly Payments**

_____**% Average Interest Rate**

C - Creditor   BO - Balance Owed
R - Rate   AC – Avail. Credit
T - Terms   MP - Min. Payment

1. C _____   BO $_____

   R _____   AC $_____

   T _____   MP $_____

2. C _____   BO $_____

   R _____   AC $_____

   T _____   MP $_____

3. C _____   BO $_____

   R _____   AC $_____

   T _____   MP $_____

4. C _____   BO $_____

   R _____   AC $_____

   T _____   MP $_____

5. C _____   BO $_____

   R _____   AC $_____

   T _____   MP $_____

6. C _____   BO $_____

   R _____   AC $_____

   T _____   MP $_____

7. C _____   BO $_____

   R _____   AC $_____

   T _____   MP $_____

Totals:

$_____ in Balance Owed

$_____ in Monthly Payments

_____% Average Interest Rate

C - Creditor   **BO - Balance Owed**
R - Rate   **AC – Avail. Credit**
T - Terms   **MP - Min. Payment**

1. **C** _____ **BO** $_____

   R _____ **AC** $_____

   T _____ **MP** $_____

2. **C** _____ **BO** $_____

   R _____ **AC** $_____

   T _____ **MP** $_____

3. **C** _____ **BO** $_____

   R _____ **AC** $_____

   T _____ **MP** $_____

4. **C** _____ **BO** $_____

   R _____ **AC** $_____

   T _____ **MP** $_____

5. C_____   BO $_____

    R_____   AC $_____

    T_____   MP $_____

6. C_____   BO $_____

    R_____   AC $_____

    T_____   MP $_____

7. C_____   BO $_____

    R_____   AC $_____

    T_____   MP $_____

Totals:

$_____ **in Balance Owed**

$_____ **in Monthly Payments**

_____**% Average Interest Rate**

C - Creditor   BO - Balance Owed
R - Rate   AC – Avail. Credit
T - Terms   MP - Min. Payment

1. C _____ BO $_____

   R _____ AC $_____

   T _____ MP $_____

2. C _____ BO $_____

   R _____ AC $_____

   T _____ MP $_____

3. C _____ BO $_____

   R _____ AC $_____

   T _____ MP $_____

4. C _____ BO $_____

   R _____ AC $_____

   T _____ MP $_____

5. **C** _____ **BO** \$_____

   R _____ **AC** \$_____

   T _____ **MP** \$_____

6. **C** _____ **BO** \$_____

   R _____ **AC** \$_____

   T _____ **MP** \$_____

7. **C** _____ **BO** \$_____

   R _____ **AC** \$_____

   T _____ **MP** \$_____

Totals:

\$_____ **in Balance Owed**

\$_____ **in Monthly Payments**

_____% **Average Interest Rate**

C - Creditor   BO - Balance Owed
R - Rate   AC – Avail. Credit
T - Terms   MP - Min. Payment

1. C _____   BO $_____

   R _____   AC $_____

   T _____   MP $_____

2. C _____   BO $_____

   R _____   AC $_____

   T _____   MP $_____

3. C _____   BO $_____

   R _____   AC $_____

   T _____   MP $_____

4. C _____   BO $_____

   R _____   AC $_____

   T _____   MP $_____

5. **C** _____ **BO** $_____

   R _____ **AC** $_____

   T _____ **MP** $_____

6. **C** _____ **BO** $_____

   R _____ **AC** $_____

   T _____ **MP** $_____

7. **C** _____ **BO** $_____

   R _____ **AC** $_____

   T _____ **MP** $_____

Totals:

$_____ **in Balance Owed**

$_____ **in Monthly Payments**

_____**% Average Interest Rate**

C - Creditor   BO - Balance Owed
R - Rate   AC – Avail. Credit
T - Terms   MP - Min. Payment

1. **C** _____   **BO** $_____

   R _____   **AC** $_____

   T _____   **MP** $_____

2. **C** _____   **BO** $_____

   R _____   **AC** $_____

   T _____   **MP** $_____

3. **C** _____   **BO** $_____

   R _____   **AC** $_____

   T _____   **MP** $_____

4. **C** _____   **BO** $_____

   R _____   **AC** $_____

   T _____   **MP** $_____

5. C_____   BO $_____

   R_____   AC $_____

   T_____   MP $_____

6. C_____   BO $_____

   R_____   AC $_____

   T_____   MP $_____

7. C_____   BO $_____

   R_____   AC $_____

   T_____   MP $_____

Totals:

$_____ in Balance Owed

$_____ in Monthly Payments

_____% Average Interest Rate

C - Creditor   BO - Balance Owed
R - Rate   AC – Avail. Credit
T - Terms   MP - Min. Payment

1. C _____   BO $_____

   R _____   AC $_____

   T _____   MP $_____

2. C _____   BO $_____

   R _____   AC $_____

   T _____   MP $_____

3. C _____   BO $_____

   R _____   AC $_____

   T _____   MP $_____

4. C _____   BO $_____

   R _____   AC $_____

   T _____   MP $_____

5. C _____ BO $_____

   R _____ AC $_____

   T _____ MP $_____

6. C _____ BO $_____

   R _____ AC $_____

   T _____ MP $_____

7. C _____ BO $_____

   R _____ AC $_____

   T _____ MP $_____

Totals:

$_____ in Balance Owed

$_____ in Monthly Payments

_____% Average Interest Rate

C - Creditor	BO - Balance Owed
R - Rate	AC – Avail. Credit
T - Terms	MP - Min. Payment

1. C _____   BO \$_____

    R _____   AC \$_____

    T _____   MP \$_____

2. C _____   BO \$_____

    R _____   AC \$_____

    T _____   MP \$_____

3. C _____   BO \$_____

    R _____   AC \$_____

    T _____   MP \$_____

4. C _____   BO \$_____

    R _____   AC \$_____

    T _____   MP \$_____

5. C_____ BO $_____

   R_____ AC $_____

   T_____ MP $_____

6. C_____ BO $_____

   R_____ AC $_____

   T_____ MP $_____

7. C_____ BO $_____

   R_____ AC $_____

   T_____ MP $_____

Totals:

$_____ in Balance Owed

$_____ in Monthly Payments

_____% Average Interest Rate

C - Creditor   **BO - Balance Owed**
R - Rate   **AC – Avail. Credit**
T - Terms   **MP - Min. Payment**

1. **C** _____   **BO** $_____

    R _____   **AC** $_____

    T _____   **MP** $_____

2. **C** _____   **BO** $_____

    R _____   **AC** $_____

    T _____   **MP** $_____

3. **C** _____   **BO** $_____

    R _____   **AC** $_____

    T _____   **MP** $_____

4. **C** _____   **BO** $_____

    R _____   **AC** $_____

    T _____   **MP** $_____

5. **C** _____ **BO** $_____

   R _____ **AC** $_____

   T _____ **MP** $_____

6. **C** _____ **BO** $_____

   R _____ **AC** $_____

   T _____ **MP** $_____

7. **C** _____ **BO** $_____

   R _____ **AC** $_____

   T _____ **MP** $_____

Totals:

$_____ in Balance Owed

$_____ in Monthly Payments

_____% Average Interest Rate

C - Creditor   **BO - Balance Owed**
R - Rate   **AC – Avail. Credit**
T - Terms   **MP - Min. Payment**

1. **C** _____ **BO** $_____

 R _____ **AC** $_____

 T _____ **MP** $_____

2. **C** _____ **BO** $_____

 R _____ **AC** $_____

 T _____ **MP** $_____

3. **C** _____ **BO** $_____

 R _____ **AC** $_____

 T _____ **MP** $_____

4. **C** _____ **BO** $_____

 R _____ **AC** $_____

 T _____ **MP** $_____

5. **C** _____   **BO** $_____

  R _____   **AC** $_____

  T _____   **MP** $_____

6. **C** _____   **BO** $_____

  R _____   **AC** $_____

  T _____   **MP** $_____

7. **C** _____   **BO** $_____

  R _____   **AC** $_____

  T _____   **MP** $_____

Totals:

$_____ **in Balance Owed**

$_____ **in Monthly Payments**

_____ **% Average Interest Rate**

C - Creditor   BO - Balance Owed
R - Rate   AC – Avail. Credit
T - Terms   MP - Min. Payment

1. C _____   BO $_____

   R _____   AC $_____

   T _____   MP $_____

2. C _____   BO $_____

   R _____   AC $_____

   T _____   MP $_____

3. C _____   BO $_____

   R _____   AC $_____

   T _____   MP $_____

4. C _____   BO $_____

   R _____   AC $_____

   T _____   MP $_____

5. C_____ BO $_____

   R_____ AC $_____

   T_____ MP $_____

6. C_____ BO $_____

   R_____ AC $_____

   T_____ MP $_____

7. C_____ BO $_____

   R_____ AC $_____

   T_____ MP $_____

Totals:

$_____ in Balance Owed

$_____ in Monthly Payments

_____% Average Interest Rate

C - Creditor   BO - Balance Owed
R - Rate   AC – Avail. Credit
T - Terms   MP - Min. Payment

1. C _____   BO $_____

   R _____   AC $_____

   T _____   MP $_____

2. C _____   BO $_____

   R _____   AC $_____

   T _____   MP $_____

3. C _____   BO $_____

   R _____   AC $_____

   T _____   MP $_____

4. C _____   BO $_____

   R _____   AC $_____

   T _____   MP $_____

5. C_____ BO $_____

   R_____ AC $_____

   T_____ MP $_____

6. C_____ BO $_____

   R_____ AC $_____

   T_____ MP $_____

7. C_____ BO $_____

   R_____ AC $_____

   T_____ MP $_____

Totals:

$_____ in Balance Owed

$_____ in Monthly Payments

_____% Average Interest Rate

C - Creditor   **BO - Balance Owed**
R - Rate   **AC – Avail. Credit**
T - Terms   **MP - Min. Payment**

1. **C** _____ **BO** $_____

 R _____ **AC** $_____

 T _____ **MP** $_____

2. **C** _____ **BO** $_____

 R _____ **AC** $_____

 T _____ **MP** $_____

3. **C** _____ **BO** $_____

 R _____ **AC** $_____

 T _____ **MP** $_____

4. **C** _____ **BO** $_____

 R _____ **AC** $_____

 T _____ **MP** $_____

5. **C** _____ **BO** $_____

   R _____ **AC** $_____

   T _____ **MP** $_____

6. **C** _____ **BO** $_____

   R _____ **AC** $_____

   T _____ **MP** $_____

7. **C** _____ **BO** $_____

   R _____ **AC** $_____

   T _____ **MP** $_____

Totals:

$_____ **in Balance Owed**

$_____ **in Monthly Payments**

_____**% Average Interest Rate**

C - Creditor   BO - Balance Owed
R - Rate   AC – Avail. Credit
T - Terms   MP - Min. Payment

1. C _____   BO $_____

   R _____   AC $_____

   T _____   MP $_____

2. C _____   BO $_____

   R _____   AC $_____

   T _____   MP $_____

3. C _____   BO $_____

   R _____   AC $_____

   T _____   MP $_____

4. C _____   BO $_____

   R _____   AC $_____

   T _____   MP $_____

5. **C** _____ **BO** $_____

   R _____ **AC** $_____

   T _____ **MP** $_____

6. **C** _____ **BO** $_____

   R _____ **AC** $_____

   T _____ **MP** $_____

7. **C** _____ **BO** $_____

   R _____ **AC** $_____

   T _____ **MP** $_____

Totals:

$_____ **in Balance Owed**

$_____ **in Monthly Payments**

_____% **Average Interest Rate**

Made in the USA
Charleston, SC
25 February 2012